FORENSIC SCIENCE

Stopping Counterfeit Crime

Richard Spilsbury

FRANKLIN WATTS
LONDON•SYDNEY

This edition first published in 2010
by Franklin Watts
338 Euston Road
London NW1 3BH

Franklin Watts Australia
Level 17/207 Kent Street
Sydney, NSW 2000

A CIP catalogue record for this book is
available from the British Library.

ISBN: 978 0 7496 9504 0

Dewey number: 363.3'59334

Printed in Malaysia

Franklin Watts is a division of
Hachette Children's Books,
an Hachette UK company.
www.hachette.co.uk

Note to parents and teachers
concerning websites:
In the book every effort has been made by
the Publishers to ensure that websites are
suitable for children, that they are of the
highest educational value, and that they
contain no inappropriate or offensive
material. However, because of the nature of
the Internet, it is impossible to guarantee that
the contents of these sites will not be altered.
We advise that Internet access is supervised by
a responsible adult.

For The Brown Reference Group Ltd
Project Editor: Sarah Eason
Designer: Paul Myerscough
Picture Researcher: Maria Joannou
Managing Editor: Miranda Smith
Editorial Director: Lindsey Lowe
Production Director: Alastair Gourlay
Children's Publisher: Anne O'Daly

Contents

Making fakes

Criminals around the world create fake objects and sell them to other people. They do this to make money, even though it cheats other people, organisations and even governments.

What is a counterfeit?

A counterfeit is a copy of something that is made to fool people into thinking it is real. For example, you may go to a shop and try to buy something with a £10 note. It looks like any other £10 note, but the shop will not let you use it because they discover it is a counterfeit. You cannot spend a worthless fake. You have been deceived into thinking it is real. So, you have been cheated out of £10 by the criminals who made the counterfeit.

A forensic scientist examines a forged painting under a microscope. An expert eye can pick out areas of retouched paint.

IN DEPTH

Range of counterfeits

Almost anything that has monetary value has been counterfeited at some point. Here are some of the most commonly counterfeited goods:

- currency such as pounds and euros
- identity documents such as passports and driver's licences
- designer goods such as clothing, perfume and watches
- medicines and drugs
- works of art such as paintings
- CDs, DVDs and computer software

Billions of euro fake notes are seized every year.

Master copiers

Forgery is the process of making or changing documents or other objects into counterfeits. Forgers are often skilled at copying real objects. For example, an art forger may paint pictures just like those of a famous painter, such as Picasso. Forgery is not illegal in itself. It becomes illegal when someone tries to pretend that the fake is the real thing. The art forger who sells his or her forgery as if it were actually created by Picasso is committing a crime. Crimes that involve deception such as this are known as fraud.

Fighting fraud

The global trade in counterfeit goods is estimated at around six per cent of all trade, worth hundreds of billions of pounds every year. Many people are trying to stop counterfeit trade. Forensic scientists are trained to spot fakes. They use many different kinds of technology to help them find evidence. This can help the police to arrest the counterfeiters. It can also be used by customs officers, who help to control the flow of goods between countries.

Money under the spotlight

Every fake banknote (paper money) represents a theft of real money. Police work with forensic teams to find counterfeit money and remove it from circulation. They try to catch the criminals who commit this form of fraud and convict them. The job is difficult because worldwide there are tens of millions of pounds' worth of fake money mixed in among real money. The fake money is constantly exchanged for goods, mostly without the knowledge of the person spending it.

If you suspect that a banknote may be a fake, hand it in to the police.

How professional forgers work

Professional forgers use printing plates to make counterfeit money. A different plate is used for each colour on the original note. The forgers find ink and paper that match those used for originals. It takes great skill to create printing plates. Criminals employ trained print workers in different parts of the world.

Amateur notes

People who are inexperienced in creating fake money are called amateur forgers. They use colour photocopiers, scanners and computer printers to create fake paper money. This equipment is widely available and easy to use. However, the copies produced are not very accurate and usually do not fool many people.

Real money is printed onto cotton paper, which gives a perfect finish. It is easy to spot money printed onto copier paper – the ink is often blotchy and the images may be blurred.

TRUE CRIME...

Operation Bernhard

During World War II, the Nazi Party developed a plan called Operation Bernhard. The plan was to distribute fake money for use in Britain and the United States. If people spent these counterfeit banknotes, the value of real money would fall, which would weaken the economies of Britain and the United States. The Nazis trained 142 forgers to make millions of US and British banknotes. By the time they had created perfect forgeries, the war had ended. The Nazis dumped the fake money into a German lake, and it was discovered there in the 1950s.

IN THE LAB

The fibre of money

One way that forensic scientists determine if currency is real is by fibre analysis. UK banknotes are made from cotton fibre and linen rag. These fibres give the notes greater strength and flexibility than the more common wood pulp paper fibres. Most countries use paper from a particular paper factory. Each factory uses fibres that are slightly different. For example, some fibres are fluorescent (they glow in the dark) when viewed in ultraviolet light. Security measures such as these are very difficult to copy. Scientists examine the shape and colour of fibres to ensure the money is genuine.

▲ *A watermark shows up best when a note is held up to the light.*

Difficult to copy

A £20 note may not look like anything more than an image printed on a small rectangle of paper. But there is more to it than meets the eye. The Royal Mint makes real banknotes. It adds different security features to make it very difficult to copy the notes. These features are easily spotted by experts such as bank workers and forensic scientists. If the security features are missing, or are wrong, the money is fake.

Here are a few of the security features found in banknotes:

Watermarks are a distinctive design created within the paper when it is made, rather than being printed on top of the paper. They are usually invisible but show up when you hold the note up to the light.

Holograms are patterns that resemble three-dimensional objects, such as a face, when viewed from certain angles. Holograms are usually found in embossed (raised) circles or other shapes that look as if they are made of silver foil.

Printed images have some lines so fine and delicate that it would be impossible for a photocopier or scanner to read them and so reproduce them. These lines may appear blurred if copied, which shows that the note is a fake.

EXAMINE THE EVIDENCE

Money studies

Can you spot some of the security features on different banknotes? Collect some currency from a few different countries – you could ask your friends or relatives who have travelled. Use a desk lamp and a magnifying glass to examine the notes for fibres, holograms, watermarks and other features. Which features would be hardest for a counterfeiter to fake?

9

Printing serial numbers that are unique to each note can help to prevent banknote forgery.

Making safer banknotes

Since 1996, the United States Treasury has created new currency with improved security measures to make dollar bills harder to forge. In 2008, the Treasury issued a new $5 bill.

On the surface

Artists prepare the printing plates by cutting the image of the $5 bill into the metal. This process is called engraving. The plate is covered with sticky ink and then rubbed clean, leaving ink only in the grooves. The printing press pushes the plate firmly onto the paper, which pushes the paper down except in the grooves where the ink remains. In this way, the printed lines are raised above the rest of the banknote. A forgery will rarely have raised lines such as these.

The new $5 bill has many special security features that are easier for people to check.

Printing the detail

Some of the lines in the image on the $5 bill are incredibly fine.
They are so fine that a photocopier or scanner will not recognise
them as separate lines, so they will come out blurred
if copied. In fact, some of the lines are strings of tiny words
that can be seen only through a strong magnifying glass. For
example, 'USA FIVE' is printed on the lower '5' of the $5 bill.

Spot the colour!

The $5 bill is printed with a special ink that can change colour
from green to black. It can do this because tiny metal flakes
are added to the ink. The metal flakes reflect light differently
depending on the angle at which you look at the bill, creating
the different colours. Only the US Treasury is able to buy
the materials that make up this special ink.

Using the thread

New $5 bills have security threads made of thin foil, or plastic
strips, embedded in the paper. Genuine threads glow blue under
ultraviolet light. The thread is in different places on bills of
different values, so forgers cannot remove the '5' thread from
a $5 bill and replace
it with a '20'
thread. Even if
the new lettering
looks genuine,
the position of
the thread shows
that the note is
a counterfeit.

11

*Officials from the
Federal Reserve
Bank announce
the launch of the
new $5 bill in
Washington DC
in 2008.*

Copying coins

Around the world, billions of coins are in use every day. There are also thousands of old coins that are no longer used for payment but are traded and collected by enthusiasts. Many of these coins – both old and new – are fakes.

Making fakes

Forging coins is not a new idea. The earliest coins were made from precious metals such as gold and silver. Forgers created fake coins by coating cheaper metals with a thin layer of the precious metal or by mixing other metals to look like the metal. Today's forgers often copy images and words stamped onto real coins to make moulds. Then they pour molten (melted) metal into the moulds to make casts of the originals.

Unlike banknotes, few people bother to check change given in coins. Making counterfeit coins can be very profitable for criminals.

Metal matters

Different types of coin are made from different metals. For example, the British 1p and 2p coins are made from copper-plated steel. The 5p, 10p and 50p coins are made from cupronickel (75 per cent copper and 25 per cent nickel). The 20p coin is also made from cupronickel, but with 84 per cent copper and 16 per cent nickel. Each type of coin also has a particular size and weight of metal. For example, a 1p coin weighs 3.56 grams and a 2p weighs 7.12 grams.

Collectors will pay a high price to buy old, rare coins. The price is often much higher than their value when they were being used.

Spotting fakes

Fake coins are fairly easy to spot. Casts are obvious because tiny air bubbles form when the molten metal cools. Fakes that are stamped onto metal often have a less detailed image that may not be centred on the coin. Reeds are the narrow bars around the edge of some coins. Other coins have inscriptions around the edge. Reeds and inscriptions are tricky to fake, because the edge of a coin is so narrow.

Electronic coin testers

Modern ticket and vending machines can identify fake coins automatically! When you put a coin in the slot, it passes through an electric field. Only coins made of the right-sized piece of the correct metal conduct the right amount of electricity. In a second test, coins are made to roll past a magnet. The magnet attracts the metal and slows down the rolling coin. Sensors in the vending machine detect the change in speed. Each type of coin changes speed by a different amount. Fake coins will usually fail one or both of these tests.

Dangerous counterfeits

C riminals around the world also make and sell counterfeit medicines. According to the World Health Organisation (WHO), 10 per cent of all medicines for sale are counterfeit. Fake medicines can be dangerous because they may make people sicker or even kill them. They are also not as effective as real medicines, so people do not get better.

Types of fake medicine

Criminals make and sell many different fake medicines to treat all kinds of disease, from AIDS to malaria. Malaria is one of the world's biggest killer diseases. It is passed on by some types of female mosquito when they bite people. Chemicals in real anti-malarial drugs, such as artesunate, are used to treat severe malaria after it has developed in a person.

The active ingredient

The chemical that makes a medicine effective is described as the 'active ingredient'. Fake drugs contain less

A forensic chemist uses a microscope to examine traces of chemicals taken from a batch of fake drugs.

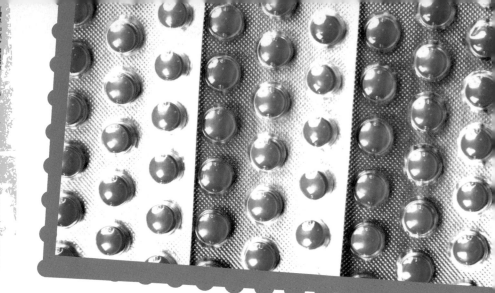

The Internet has opened up the market for fake drugs. This makes it hard to track down the people who commit counterfeit crimes.

(or none) of the expensive active ingredients, but the buyer still pays the price of the genuine medicine. Using too little of the active ingredient found in the original drug to treat malaria makes treatment using the fake medicine ineffective.

Finding the fakes

Forensic chemists find out which chemicals are used to make fake drugs. They use a wide range of chemical tests and devices such as spectroscopes to test drugs. These measure how the chemicals in the drugs respond to electricity, heat or light. The chemists also test the medicines by adding different chemicals that react with the active ingredients. This often creates a change in their colour or in their weight.

TRUE CRIME...

Trading fakes

In 2006, Chinese authorities arrested a man in southern China for selling fake anti-malarial drugs. Forensic chemists bought the fake artesunate tablets from different chemists across Southeast Asia. After the drugs were analysed, forensic chemists revealed that 38 per cent of the samples had no artesunate in them at all. Most had too little to fight malaria effectively. Scientists found tiny amounts of pollen in the tablets as having come from southern China. They then tracked down the factory where the counterfeit tablets were made.

Fake luxuries

Many people like to buy luxury items, such as jewellery, perfumes and designer clothes and bags. They are prepared to pay a lot more to buy the very best. However, criminals produce cheap copies of these luxury brands to fool people into buying them. Forensics experts are vital in the job of spotting the counterfeit goods and in helping the police to catch the forgers.

Making fake perfumes

Genuine perfumes are made by expert perfume blenders. They may mix together hundreds of different scents to create a unique blend. Some forgers try to mimic the original perfume using unusual ingredients. For example, some fake perfumes have been found

A forensic scientist tests a perfume to see if the chemicals from which it is made match those found in the genuine item.

Electronic nose

Laboratory analysis of perfume is time-consuming. A Brazilian scientist has developed a system that can analyse a scent in just two minutes. It is a portable machine that compares the chemical signature of vapour from a real scent with that of a fake. The signature shows the proportions of different chemicals used to make the perfume and should be the same in every bottle of genuine fragrance. Counterfeit versions have different signatures, because rarely are forgers able to match the original exactly.

Street traders often sell big-name brands of watches at bargain prices. These items are usually fakes.

to contain pond water and even goat's urine! These unpleasant ingredients were chosen to provide musky smells in the counterfeit scent. A bigger problem is when forgers use chemicals that can be harmful to people. Some of the chemicals in fake perfumes give people skin rashes.

Identifying fake perfumes

Some fake perfumes are easy to spot. They may be packed in poorly printed wrapping. They may be sold on the street, rather than in well-known shops. Other fake perfumes are presented quite professionally. To stop the cheats, some perfume companies add packaging tags that contain tiny particles that can be identified under a microscope. However, the only way to identify some fake perfumes is to have their contents analysed by forensic scientists. One test is to heat up the perfume. Different substances in the liquid evaporate at different temperatures. Scientists condense the vapours (gases) in cooled tubes and then identify the separate liquids.

Precious gems

To make counterfeit jewellery, crooks make fake gems that look like the genuine items. They use machines to turn hard plastic or glass into fake diamonds, emeralds or other gems. They may even create doublets, which are chunks of cheap stone with a thin slice of the real gem on top. Forensic scientists test the gems in different ways. For example, a genuine diamond cannot be scratched with anything but another diamond or a diamond-coated blade.

18

Garments and bags

Fake clothes, handbags and shoes are widely available from markets, the Internet and even major shops. They are usually copies of goods made by popular sports brands, such as Adidas or Nike, or expensive designer brands such as Chanel or Gucci. Criminals who create these goods rely on the public easily recognising their brand names, logos and designs.

Crooks are waiting to make copies of designer clothes almost as soon as the fashion shows are over.

TRUE CRIME...

Shoe scam

In July 2003, police seized 25 truckloads of Nike and Adidas shoe parts from assembly shops in Ho Chi Minh City in Vietnam. Working on a tip-off from Nike, Vietnamese authorities had uncovered a 'leakage' scam. Workers in a genuine Nike factory had stolen defective shoe parts. They had sold them to assembly shops, where workers were mending or disguising the defective parts. They were then using the parts to make fake shoes to export to other countries.

↑ *An expert can tell if a gem is genuine by examining it under a magnifying glass called a loupe.*

Some fake garments are simply mass-produced, poor-quality items with a fake designer label stuck onto them. Others are lookalikes. These are well-made copies of an original that are sold with a different label. For example, some garments feature a chequered pattern very similar to the characteristic design used on expensive Burberry clothing.

Other fakes are actually originals! Some designer bags sold cheaply on the street are made in the same factories, using the same materials and designs as those sold in expensive shops. Criminals may bribe the factories to let them have the bags cheaply, then sell them at a higher price.

EXAMINE THE EVIDENCE

Beneath the label

Look at some branded goods such as clothes, perfumes and shoes in your home or at your local market. Can you tell if they are fakes or genuine items? Some tell-tale clues on fake clothes include peel-off brand labels, labels with spelling mistakes or having no label showing where the garment was made.

Pirated copies

Counterfeit CDs and DVDs are known as pirated copies. They are widely available on the Internet, from mail-order shops and from market traders. Many people are happy to pay much less than in the shops to see a new film on a pirated DVD or hear the latest tracks on a fake CD. This is illegal. Criminals around the world earn at least £2.9 billion from music piracy each year.

Pirated DVDs are much cheaper than the original DVDs, but the quality of the recording is often terrible.

Piracy problems

When people buy an album or film, part of the money goes to the artist as a royalty. Pirated copies generate no royalties, and fewer copies of the genuine items are sold. Pirated computer software causes companies and shops to lose around £7.5 billion each year. China and Vietnam are hotspots for the production of pirated computer software.

Getting the data

Criminals get the data for pirated DVDs from several different kinds of source. They may get copies of originals from people who work in film studios or software houses. They may download files from file-sharing sites on the Internet. They may also make illegal recordings of original works. Some pirated DVDs are created by recording a film on a video camera in a cinema!

Finding fault

Most pirated copies are easy to spot. The cover may be poorly printed or have spelling mistakes. The quality may also be poor, with blurred images and poor sound, sometimes in the wrong language. Recording companies often try to stop criminals by putting coded information on DVDs to prevent them from being copied.

TRUE CRIME...

DrinkorDie

In February 2002, 28-year-old John Sankus Jr of Philadelphia was sentenced to 46 months in prison for leading an international piracy ring called DrinkorDie. This group of about 60 people from the United States, Australia, Norway and other countries illegally copied and distributed computer software. Computers belonging to some DrinkorDie members contained enough hacked software to fill 700,000 disks.

21

Criminals burn genuine software onto blank disks and sell the pirated copies for huge profits.

Suspicious spares

Many machines have parts that can be replaced when they wear out. Spare parts include batteries, light bulbs, memory cards, tyres and windscreens. Criminals make cheap copies of genuine spares, because the global trade in fake spares is big business. Car manufacturers estimate that the loss of sales in genuine spare parts costs them around £7.5 billion each year. This is enough money for the industry to employ an extra 200,000 workers!

Fitting cars with counterfeit parts is very dangerous. The parts could fail and cause the car to crash.

Spare appeal

Spares are always in demand, because parts wear out or fail. When companies need a spare part, they may not have time to shop around. When a truck is not in use because it is waiting for new tyres, for example, a haulage company cannot carry as many goods and so loses money. Fake spares that look like the real thing are cheap to make. People are naturally attracted by parts that are cheaper than usual.

Dangerous batteries

Batteries are made of chemicals that react to produce electricity. Forgers sometimes use the wrong chemicals when they make batteries. The reaction between these chemicals makes electricity, but it can also produce lots of heat. Overheating batteries can affect the parts inside battery-operated devices, from mobile phones to MP3 players. Overheating can even make the device explode!

Fake batteries present a fire hazard because they can overheat.

Dangerous fakes

Fakes may look like the real thing, but they do not always work properly and can be dangerous. Sometimes you can spot a fake by the differences in the packaging. Fake items often become obvious only after things have gone wrong. In one example, forensic investigators realised that fires under cars were being caused by a fake brand of brake pad. Real brake pads are coated with metal filings that rub against discs inside the wheels to slow down the cars. The pads on the cars that caught fire were fakes. They were coated with sawdust and grass and sprayed to look like metal. The heat caused by braking set the pads on fire.

TRUE CRIME...

Fakes in the sky!

In the late 1970s, fake aeroplane parts were discovered that could have cost lives. The parts were pumps used to fold the landing wheels in and out of Boeing 727 and 737 aeroplanes. The fake pumps were made from a chrome-covered steel rather than solid chrome. Solid chrome does not rust, but steel does. If the fake spares had been used, the chrome would have chipped off and the metal below would have rusted. Without pumps to operate the landing wheels, the aeroplanes would have undoubtedly crashed.

Looking closely at art

The most valuable works of art by the best artists sell for millions of pounds. With so much money at stake, criminals commission talented artists to fake copies of paintings, drawings and sculptures. If the fakes can fool the experts and sell as the genuine items, the criminals can pocket a lot of money. Art experts and forensic scientists use their knowledge to uncover fakes and help to find the criminals responsible.

The auction house Sotheby's offers a Picasso for sale in 2008. Art experts claim that one or two out of every ten works of art sold at auction are fakes.

Forging art

There is a wide range of fake art for sale. Some forgeries are clumsy copies of real art. Other forgeries are good copies in the style of famous artists or periods in art. Forgers use different techniques to make their images look older. For example, they paint on old pieces of canvas, or they age frames by drilling 'insect' holes in the wood. Some forgers use chemicals such as acids on the paint to age the paintings.

A close view

A scanning electron microscope fires an invisible beam of tiny particles, called electrons, over the surface of a sample such as paint. Signals are produced when the electrons hit chemicals in the sample. A detector converts the signals into an image on a screen. Different chemicals produce different signals, so the images show which chemicals are in the sample.

A forensic scientist removes a sample of paint from a work of art. The chemicals in paint have changed over time, so this often reveals a forgery.

25

Finding faults

Art experts often find fakes using their expert knowledge of real artists. Some famous artists have distinctive brush strokes. Marks on a sculpture made with modern tools look different from those made with the tools available in the past. Experts also examine the history of paintings. They look at auction house records to track when a work of art has been bought and sold.

Forensic finds

Forensic scientists remove tiny samples of paint, stone, canvas, paper or other material from a work of art to test it. They analyse

IN DEPTH

Unseen image

To X-ray a painting, a sheet of film is placed behind it. A machine fires X-rays through the canvas. X-rays will move through some paint colours more easily than others. An image is created on the film, showing the different layers of paint used on the canvas. X-ray images called radiographs can also reveal artists' signatures, sketches behind a painting and even fingerprints.

Laboratories in the ➡
world's major art
galleries use X-ray
analysis to ensure that
every work of art in their
collection is genuine.

the type and age of the chemicals in the samples using scanning electron microscopes. Materials such as paint have changed over time. A painter from the past could use only materials that were available at that particular time. For example, if a painting that is supposedly from medieval times includes Prussian blue paint, it must be a fake. This is because Prussian blue paint was not invented until 1704, more than two centuries after the medieval period ended.

Seeing through paintings

Many old paintings were created on previously used canvases or pieces of wood, because these materials were expensive or rare. Sometimes artists painted over other images. Forensic scientists can use X-rays to see these hidden images without damaging the paint. This can help them to work out if a painting is genuine. For example, a painting was discovered recently that experts believed was painted by Pablo Picasso in the 19th century.

Scientists found that it was painted over another painting in the abstract style. The picture was a fake, because abstract art did not exist until the 20th century.

Confusing the experts

Identifying a work of art as a fake is hard. For example, the French artist Jean Corot and the American artist Andy Warhol signed copies of their works that were actually made by other people they hired to work for them. Also, over time paintings become damaged or dirty. Restorers may clean them up and even add or remove details. Forensic scientists may then conclude that some materials are fake while others are original within the same work of art. Some 'fakes' are later proved to be genuine by the use of newer art analysis techniques.

Shaun Greenhalgh (left) fooled the art world for many years with the help of his parents, George (centre) and Olive (right).

TRUE CRIME...

Fake family

In 1997, The Art Institute of Chicago bought a small sculpture for £78,000. Experts said that it was made by the famous French artist Paul Gauguin. It was later proved to be an expert forgery. It was one of many counterfeit works of art made by a family of three forgers. The Greenhalgh family from Bolton in Britain made more than £1 million by selling fake works of art to museums and art galleries around the world. They were finally caught when a museum worker noticed a spelling mistake in an 'ancient' stone tablet and realised it was a fake. Forensic workers eventually traced the tablet back to the Greenhalghs. Shaun Greenhalgh was found guilty of fraud and jailed in 2006.

27

Foiling a forger

Han van Meegeren from the Netherlands was one of the most famous art forgers of all time. He created paintings in the style of the 17th-century Dutch master, Johannes Vermeer. Van Meegeren sold his fake Vermeers in the 1930s and 1940s. He pretended that the paintings were newly discovered originals. Many experts were fooled, because van Meegeren was very good at painting and at making his counterfeits look old.

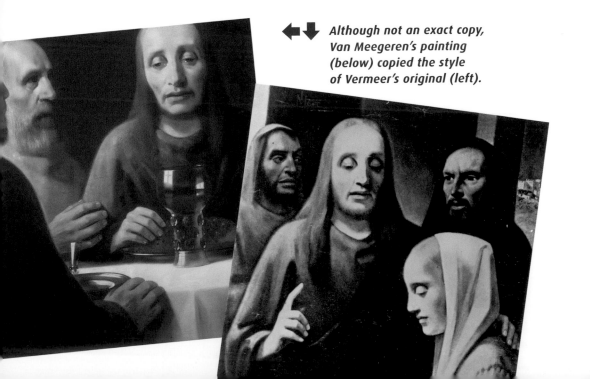

Although not an exact copy, Van Meegeren's painting (below) copied the style of Vermeer's original (left).

Han van Meegeren was sentenced to one year in prison for his forgeries, but he died before the sentence could be served.

Expert faker

Here are some of the steps that van Meegeren used to create his fakes.

Canvas

He bought genuine 17th-century paintings that he then cleaned with a pumice stone and water.

Paint and brushes

He mixed up his own paints from raw materials that would have been available in the 17th century. He painted using brushes made of badger hair, similar to those used by Vermeer.

Cracking

Once he had painted a canvas, he used a chemical to dry the paint and baked it to make it dry harder. Finally, he rolled up the canvas to crack the paint.

Study

Van Meegeren knew that historians thought Vermeer had travelled to Italy to study the art there. So he painted pictures with themes based on those of 17th-century Italian artists, such as Caravaggio.

The mistake

Art dealers became suspicious about the new paintings, because it was unusual for so many works by an old master to turn up so quickly. Forensic teams soon found a mistake in a fake called *The Last Supper*. Radiographs showed a hunting scene under the image. Hunting scenes were never painted by Vermeer. Van Meegeren had failed to remove the previous painting from his old canvas.

Revising history

Historical artefacts can also be forged. These include printed materials such as old books, maps and pieces of music. Since medieval times, many fake religious relics have been identified. Many of these objects would be of great interest and value if they were genuine, so forensic scientists use various techniques to discover whether they are fakes.

Konrad Kujau (below) and the journalist who helped him to sell The Hitler Diaries *in 1981 were put in prison after forensics proved that the diaries were fake.*

Hitler's diaries

One of the most famous forgeries in history was the case of the forged diaries of Adolf Hitler, the Nazi leader of Germany during World War II. In 1981, a German newspaper spent £1.25 million on what it believed to be Hitler's personal diaries. In 1983, West German police checked the diaries using forensic analysis. Studies of the paper used in the diaries revealed a chemical and fibres that were only used years after Hitler's death. Chromatography identified four different kinds of ink that were not available when Hitler was alive. Closer analysis of the ink suggested that the diary was only a few years old!

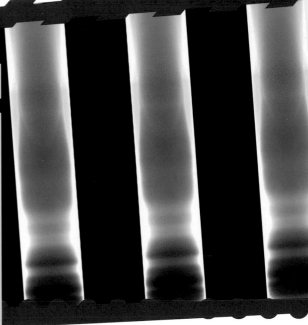

⬆ *Police use chromatography to help them solve suspected cases of forgery.*

31

Pen and ink

Chromatography is a test used to separate chemicals. Ink consists of many pigments (chemical colours). To separate the different pigments, ink is first soaked out of the paper and then put in a solvent. Ingredients other than pigments can be seen with ultraviolet or infrared light. Forensic scientists use these findings to work out the type of pen used or the date when something was written.

EXAMINE THE EVIDENCE

Chromatography

Draw a row of crosses across the middle of a paper towel with coloured, washable felt-tip pens. Hang this over a dish of water, so that the towel end touches the water. As the water soaks upwards, the inks travel with it. Halos of colour gather around the crosses. Some colour pigment molecules travel further than others. That is why some halos stay the original colour while others change colour.

↑ *The Vinland Map is an important find. It suggests that North America was discovered more than 50 years before Columbus set foot in the New World in 1492.*

Map forgeries

Map specialists use their knowledge to work out if an old map is genuine or fake. Early maps were printed by hand, one at a time, by inking an engraved copper plate or woodblock. They were coloured by hand, too, so the brush strokes are visible. An easy way to spot a fake old colour map is with a magnifying glass.

Pigments on early maps also differ. For example, maps made in medieval times were coloured using iron-based inks. These tend to break down over time, leaving yellow or brown stains. Green colours were often made using copper, which can corrode and damage the paper.

TRUE CRIME...

The Vinland Map mystery

The Vinland Map, discovered in 1957, is dated to 1440. It could be the oldest map of North America ever found. Experts disagree about whether or not the map is genuine, and they have used different methods to date it. One study looked at the inks used and found traces of titanium dioxide. This pigment was not used in inks until after the 1920s. This suggested that the map is a modern fake. In 2002, a carbon-dating study of the parchment on which the map is drawn dated it from the 15th century. In this case, though, carbon dating cannot be considered conclusive, because the map could have been drawn onto the paper at a later date.

Carbon dating

Carbon dating is a method of establishing exactly how old something is – or rather how long ago it died. Carbon dating works only on things that were once alive, such as plants and animals. This is because they contain a certain form of carbon called carbon-14. Substances such as metal cannot be dated with this technique. Carbon dating can be used to date maps made on paper, because paper comes from wood that was once a living tree.

How carbon dating works

A tiny percentage of the total carbon in any living thing is a form called carbon-14, or C-14. Scientists know that when a living thing dies, the C-14 in its body gradually starts to disappear. In fact, it takes 5,568 years for the amount of C-14 to fall by one half. By measuring the amount of C-14 in the paper of an old map and comparing it with the percentage that would originally have been there, scientists can accurately date the paper.

A forensic scientist studies a map to see if it is a fake.

Investigating the Turin Shroud

Some Christians believe that the Turin Shroud is the cloth in which Jesus Christ was wrapped and buried after he died. It shows a faint imprint of a crucified man, which some people believe is an image of Christ. The image could have been made in various ways. Perhaps it is the remains of a painting or blood and sweat that has somehow imprinted on the cloth. One test of whether or not the Turin Shroud is a fake is to find out how old it is. Can scientists prove that it is really more than 2,000 years old?

1. In 1988, three university laboratories did carbon-dating tests on pieces from one small corner of the shroud. All agreed that the fabric dated from between 1260 and 1390, which is more than 1,000 years after Jesus lived.

2. In 1993, scientist Stephen Mattingly of the University of Texas Health Science Center suggested that the 1988 carbon-dating results were wrong, because the pieces tested were contaminated with bacteria. People who handled the cloth could have left bacteria on it. He proposed that this increased the amount of C-14 and made the fabric appear younger than it really was.

3. The 1988 carbon-dating results were further discredited by Russian scientist Dmitri Kouznetsov and a Canadian–American physicist named John Jackson. They suggested that the shroud's carbon content changed when it was exposed to a fire in 1532. Smoke from the fire contaminated the cloth with the gas carbon monoxide.

4. In 2005, American chemist Raymond Rogers claimed that the bits of material that were carbon dated were not originally from the shroud. He suggested that they were from different fabric that was used to repair the shroud in medieval times.

5. In 2008, Professor Christopher Ramsey from Oxford University in England tested some linen samples from the shroud and confirmed the smoke contamination. Further tests in the future may finally solve the mystery of the shroud.

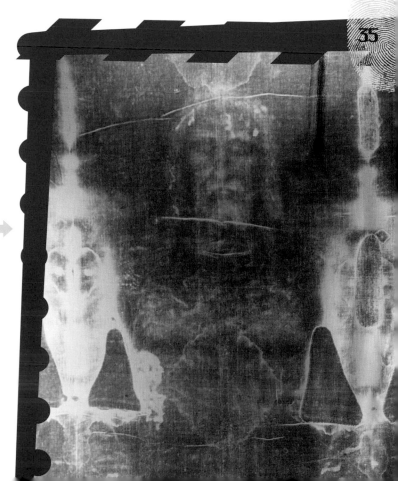

The Turin Shroud was found in France in the 14th century. Since 1578, it has been stored safely in a cathedral in Turin, Italy. It is rarely put on public display, because exposing it to light would make it decay more rapidly.

35

Criminals may replace genuine photos in passports with those of the people who buy the fake documents.

Stealing information

There are many ways in which criminals find information to be forged, such as signatures. They may overhear people using identifying information. They may find addresses, dates of birth, bank account numbers and other personal information by looking through documents, or even old computers, thrown out in the rubbish. Criminals may steal or break into cars or houses to get information. They can even use stolen information to make completely counterfeit objects, such as credit cards and passports.

Cybercrime

One of the fastest-growing crimes today is cybercrime. Cybercrime involves using computers or the Internet to steal information and commit fraud. Criminals increasingly find out about their victims using computers. Sometimes they search the Internet for online government records or browse social-networking sites such as MySpace or Facebook.

Expert computer users can break into computer databases to steal information. This is called hacking. They may even send e-mails to their victims, pretending to be a trustworthy company or organisation. They request information on behalf of the company. This is called phishing.

Forensic techniques

Different people write in different ways. Some people press harder on the paper than others when they write. This leaves tiny impressions, or grooves, in the paper and breaks the paper fibres. Sometimes forgers lean on other documents while they copy, and this may leave impressions of their writing.

Forensic scientists look for these impressions on suspicious documents. They shine a light on the paper from an angle and view the shadows around the impressions using a stereomicroscope. This is like a very powerful magnifying glass that is used with both eyes. When the impressions are too shallow to see clearly, forensic scientists use a machine called an ESDA to look at the documents in more detail.

Even if forgers are excellent at copying a signature, they may not fool the scientists. ➡

IN DEPTH

First impressions

ESDA stands for **E**lectro**s**tatic **D**etection **A**pparatus. The scientist places a sheet of paper on the machine. The machine attaches a thin plastic film onto the paper. The film has an electrostatic charge, like the charge produced by rubbing a balloon on a sweater and then sticking it to a wall. The charge varies over the film, depending on the depth of the impressions left by the writing marks. Black ink powder sticks to the film to reveal the impressions clearly.

39

> Scanning...

.

01011011100010110010011101
10110101010011011100111101
10100111011100101010011010

.

> Identity matched
> Access granted

⬆ *A biometric scanner analyses the iris pattern of a woman's eye to confirm her identity.*

Identifying ink and paper

Sometimes criminals alter the amount of money written on a cheque, for example from £50 to £500, to get more money than was originally intended by the person who wrote the cheque. Forensic scientists can spot the differences in ink used on forged documents such as this. They use a Video Spectral Comparator (VSC). This machine shines different types of light, including infrared and ultraviolet light that our eyes cannot see, onto documents. Ink from different sources may glow or show up differently in these lights. A video camera in the VSC detects the light reflecting from the ink and displays differences in the inks on a monitor.

TRUE CRIME...

Famous forger

The most famous identity thief ever was Frank Abagnale from the United States. During the 1960s, he faked documents so that he could work as a pilot, lawyer, doctor and in other careers for which he had no training. He also forged cheques and cashed them in different countries. He made more than £1.3 million from his crimes, but he was eventually caught and imprisoned in 1971. In 1974, Abagnale was released early so that he could help the US government to catch other identity thieves. He now helps banks, companies and the FBI to stop fraud and identity theft. His life story was made into the film *Catch Me If You Can* (2002), starring Leonardo DiCaprio.

The VSC is also used by scientists to identify differences
in paper. Chemicals in paper from different sources glow
differently. Although the paper may look identical at first
glance, the equipment will reveal if it comes from a different
source. For example, a scientist can use a VSC to spot an extra
page added to a will. Such evidence may help to prove that
a criminal has committed fraud or identity theft.

Foiling identity forgers

Security workers have developed ways for people to identify
themselves without using signatures. These methods are more
difficult for criminals to forge. Smart cards have small computer
chips built into them. The chips contain data about an individual,
such as a date of birth. Some systems use biometric scanners that
are able to view unique patterns in certain parts of the body,
such as a fingerprint or the iris in the eye. If patterns are stored
in a database, identity can be proved when there is a match.

41

*A Video Spectral Comparator (VSC) can show differences
in inks and papers, which would reveal faked documents.*

writing identity

Many people have similar handwriting. A person's handwriting may look like that of his or her parents or resemble the handwriting of other people who learned to write in the same school. Yet each person's handwriting is unique. Subtle differences in the size, shape and flow of letters make it distinct.

Solving identity crimes

Forensic document examiners help to identify criminals by spotting attempts to forge or change writing. These experts look at the shape and slant of words and letters and the neatness of the writing. Document examiners look at how hard the person was pressing when writing. They see if the letters were written carefully or scrawled in a hurry. They look for repeated words or ways of putting together sentences. The way we write is often similar to how we speak. A person who makes grammatical mistakes when he or she talks will probably write that way, too.

When the baby of the famous aviator Charles Lindbergh was kidnapped in 1932, investigators solved the case by matching the handwriting in this ransom note to that of the suspect.

Building a character portrait

Graphologists make hundreds of measurements and evaluations of a sample of handwriting to create a character profile.
For example:
- heavy writing – the person may be under stress
- very small writing – may lack social confidence
- tall letters – may be ambitious
- long bar on small 't' – lively and energetic
- u-shaped bar on small 't' – may be untrustworthy, evasive.

Handwriting analysis can reveal a lot about a person's character.

43

Interpreting handwriting

Some people claim that our handwriting can reveal something about the kind of person we are. Experts who can determine the character of an individual from his or her writing are called graphologists. Graphologists may examine writing using the same tools as forensic document examiners, such as ESDA. Then they create a character portrait, which is a summary of what the writing tells them about the person who wrote the letter. Police officers may compare the character portrait with what they know about possible suspects. If there is a potential character match, they will investigate the suspect further.

However, many experts are sceptical about the conclusions reached by graphologists. The experts believe that an individual's handwriting can change because of many factors, such as age or illness. They say that graphology is completely subjective. This means that different graphologists may come up with very different interpretations of the same piece of writing.

Careers in forensics

Do you like searching for clues and solving mysteries? Do you enjoy carrying out scientific experiments for hours at a time? Are you interested in how people catch criminals? If your answers to these questions are 'yes', then you will probably enjoy a career in forensic science.

The right skills

People need the right skills to work in forensics. The most useful subjects to study at school are sciences such as chemistry and biology. At university, people may take forensics courses. A degree in forensics will include science, but it may also include courses on law and crime. Forensic scientists also need other skills, such as good communication abilities and attention to detail, because they will typically work on several different cases at the same time.

Some careers in forensic science involve laboratory work, so a background in science is essential.

Laboratory work

Many forensic scientists start work as technicians in forensic laboratories. They train under senior forensic chemists while they develop expertise. Common duties include setting up, operating and maintaining laboratory instruments and equipment. They monitor experiments, make observations and calculate and record results. Typical work may involve analysing anything from fake coins and medicines to paints and perfumes. This analytical background builds important skills for the future. As one forensic scientist says, 'It's very hard to get any kind of science work without lab experience, so getting work experience is important'.

SALARY CHART

This chart shows what some forensic scientists working in the field of counterfeit and forgery can expect to earn.

Forensic scientist	Approximate salary per year
Chemist	£32,000
Laboratory technician	£22,500
Fraud investigator	£38,800

Fraud experts

Many areas of forensics require fraud specialists – forensic scientists who are experts in finding evidence of forgery, counterfeiting and other forms of fraud. They may work directly for the police or for government agencies such as the immigration service. Some work in art galleries or history museums. Other fraud specialists, such as forensic document examiners, may work in banks, accounting firms or law offices. They may then use lab technicians to help prove that fraud has taken place. Organisations working to stop this kind of crime need receptionists, administrative assistants and other kinds of support staff. Many career opportunities exist for someone interested in forensics.

Glossary

biometric – Measurement of physical characteristics, such as fingerprints or DNA, to help identify someone.

carbon dating – Method of calculating the age of an object based on the different types of carbon inside it.

carbon monoxide – Invisible, odourless and poisonous gas produced by burning wood and other fuels.

computer chips – Silicon chips with tiny electronic circuits etched onto them.

condense – Change state from gas to liquid, usually by cooling.

contaminated – Made impure or unsafe by contact with other substances.

data – Organised information that may consist of numbers, words or images.

database – Collection of information, usually stored on a computer.

embossed – Decorated with a raised pattern.

evaporate – Change state from liquid to gas, usually by heating.

export – Sell or transfer goods or services to another country.

fluorescent – Glowing by absorbing energy and giving out light.

forensic scientist – Person who uses science and technology to investigate and establish facts in a criminal case.

forgery – Process of making or adapting objects or documents, usually with the intention of deceiving others.

fraud – Crime of deliberate deception to steal money, property or other valuable commodities.

hack – Unlawfully break into a computer system.

identity theft – Stealing personal details and using them to commit fraud.

infrared – Type of light invisible to our eyes, with wavelengths longer than visible red light.

medieval – Period in history between about 800 and 1500 CE.

phishing – Type of Internet fraud in which people are tricked into disclosing personal information, such as bank account numbers.

pigments – Substances used to give ink or paint a particular colour.

pirated – Illegally copied from an original item for sale and distribution.

pollen – Fertilising part of flowering plants, consisting of powdery, yellow grains.

printing plates – Surfaces bearing an image for transfer onto paper or other material.

royalty – Payment for the right to use someone else's creative work.

shroud – Cloth used to wrap the body of a dead person.

solvent – Liquid used for dissolving another substance to form a solution.

spectroscope – Instrument used by scientists to observe light or radiation from any source.

ultraviolet – Type of light invisible to our eyes, with wavelengths shorter than visible violet or blue light.

X-rays – Energetic rays that can pass through substances that rays of light cannot penetrate.

Further reading

Books

Cooper, Chris. *Forensic Science.* London: Dorling Kindersley, 2008.

Dowen, Elizabeth. *What's it Like to be a Forensic Scientist?* London: A & C Black Publishers, 2009.

Platt, Richard. *Forensics.* London: Kingfisher, 2008.

Webber, Diane. *Do You Read Me?: Famous Cases Solved by Handwriting Analysis!* London: Franklin Watts, 2007.

Websites

To find out more about the technology that helps scientists solve art crime visit:

http://whyfiles.org/081art_sci/5.html

There is more information about the Vinland Map, *The Hitler Diaries* and many other famous forgeries at:

www.pbs.org/wgbh/nova/vinland/fakes.html

Find out more about how British money is made and the security measures that protect it at the official website of the Royal Mint:

www.royalmint.com

Learn about how to avoid fake goods at:

www.safefromscams.co.uk/FakeGoodsScamsCategory.html